reservation for one

poems for the single woman

Alia Summers

reservation for one copyright © 2025 by Alia Summers

All rights reserved. No part of this book may be used, transmitted or reproduced in any form or means (written, electronic, mechanical, or other) without the author's prior explicit written permission and consent.

ISBN: 978-1-7382268-6-3

Cover design and artwork by Alia Summers

@aliasummerswrites

A note from the author –

This book is for all the single women who are feeling the weight of searching for love in a society that judges you for not having a partner.

The first chapter (*reservation for one*) will be very validating for those who find themselves often lonely, wishing for partnership, and disheartened by the search for love.

The second chapter (*love in the wrong generation*) captures how frustrating the current dating climate can be, and the moments when single women realize that partnership is not always the golden ticket to happiness.

The third chapter (*I'll be okay*) will remind you how powerful acceptance can be, how important it is to center yourself, and the value of pouring into your own life, even while still hoping for love.

In this book, I hoped to express the spectrum of emotions that single women face, as every moment is different and this is a truly non-linear experience. **You are allowed to feel both sad about, and empowered by, being single – perhaps even all in the same day.**

Whatever you are feeling about your singlehood on any given day, I hope you remember you are so much more than your partnership status.

contents

reservation for one....7

love in the wrong generation....47

I'll be okay....85

1. reservation for one

reservation for one

today's dating culture is full.

full of hookups,
full of games,
full of situationships,
full of disappointment.

and it's all leaving me
empty.

reservation for one

being single feels like
peace on some days,
and envy on others.

you recognize how much love
is inside of you.

you give as much as you can to yourself,
but still wish you had someone
to pour the excess into.

you hear lovers fighting,
and feel grateful for your quiet.

but you also watch them share milestones,
and you feel like you're behind.

it is the perfect balancing act
of contentment and longing.

reservation for one

I never wanted a prince charming,
and I never asked
for a knight in shining armour.

I just want someone to hold my hand,
cook dinner with,
snuggle up on the couch,
talk about our days
(the good and the bad)

someone to be there
when nobody else is.

it doesn't seem like a lot to ask for.

and yet it would mean everything to me.

reservation for one

I have been a wing-woman,
a bridesmaid,
a maid of honor,
a wedding dress shopping companion,
a bouquet catcher.

I have been everything.

except the one standing at the altar
alongside someone who wants
forever
with me.

reservation for one

I feel like I don't fit in.

there is no place for me
amongst the couples,
the mothers,
the women holding the hands of their lovers
or babies in their arms.

I feel like I stick out.

like a sore thumb –
someone who fell behind,
couldn't catch up,
never arrived.

this world wasn't made for us.

for the singles,
the solitudes,
the ones who only need
a reservation for one.

reservation for one

every day I wonder
if the reason I do not have love
is because I do not deserve love.

and though I know it can't be true,
it is a pain I can never describe.

reservation for one

another christmas alone.
another year hanging ornaments in solitude
on a tree that I put up on my own,
after hanging my stocking
and filling it myself.

another valentines where I watch couples
profess their love
in pink and red and cards and glitter
and wonder if cupid forgot about me.

another vacation witnessing pairs of two
traipse the globe together,
taking photos in front of
the eiffel tower,
the colosseum,
the mountains,
while I take solo selfies
and feel grateful that I can see the world,
but still wish I had someone to see it with.

I can feel the *alone* everywhere around me,
and there's nowhere I can go
to escape it.

reservation for one

can I admit that I'm jealous
without you judging me?

can I say
that when I pass couples in the street
or at the park
or watch them in a movie,
I want that too?

can I confess these feelings
without seeming envious
or bitter
or like I don't love myself?

because I do love myself.

I just want a love like that too.

reservation for one

my heart is tired of wanting.

wanting love,
wanting companionship,
wanting to feel whole.

my heart is tired of breaking.

breaking from loneliness,
breaking from envy,
breaking from isolation.

my heart is tired of waiting.

waiting to feel complete,
waiting to exhale,
waiting to meet its mate.

my heart is tired.

reservation for one

special occasions magnify the loneliness.

I realize how secluded I feel
every time I blow out the candles
on a birthday cake
and there's no one to share a slice with.

I know how lucky I am
to even be here –
to be making another trip around the sun –
but a part of me feels the burden
of doing it alone.

new year's eve without a kiss
feels a little less sparkly
and a little less magical.

I'm grateful to ring in another year
but still wish I could do so
with someone beside me.

special occasions magnify the loneliness,
and the loneliness makes them feel
a little less special.

reservation for one

when you are the chronically single friend,
you feel like an imposition.

you wonder if you're the third wheel –
the obligation invite,
the pity call.

it's heartbreaking.

to watch your friends connect and bond
over something you want too,
but which you feel like you'll never have.

when you are the chronically single friend,
it's hard to feel like you belong anywhere.

reservation for one

you force a smile onto your face
when you see the engagements,
the bridal showers,
the anniversary posts,
the valentines tributes,
and the endless captions that read
me and my forever wedding date.

you can say *congratulations*
to the baby announcements
and *happy birthday* at the children's parties,
and truly mean it deep down in your heart.

but you can't deny
and you can't ignore
the fact that it stings –
just a little more each time.

you are not wrong for wishing,
deep inside,
that one day,
it could be you.

reservation for one

give yourself permission
to break a little
when one by one,
your friends around you
have rings placed tenderly on their fingers
and ride off into the sunset with their loves.

you can be happy for others
while also grieving the life
you thought you'd be living by now.

- the single girl struggle

reservation for one

life is so unfair.

the one who broke me
went on to find love.

it feels like the one who broke me
was rewarded,
while I was punished.

the one who broke me –
the one who convinced me they were
the love of my life
and then proceeded to instead
blow up my life,
found the love of their life.

the one who broke me
got everything I wanted.

and I am still just broken.

reservation for one

it is exhausting to be told
you'll find love when you'll least expect it.

I haven't been expecting it for years now.

I've given up,
thrown in the towel,
succumb to the quiet.

so where is it?

reservation for one

what do I do with this love inside of me?

I love my family
and I love my friends,
but let us not pretend it's the same.

it is love, of course.
but it is a different love.

let us not pretend
that the hole in my heart
where the love of my life should be
can be filled by anyone *other*
than the love of my life.

where do I pour my adoration?
it is a fire that needs a vessel
and without one, eats me alive.

what do I do with this love inside of me?

and when will I receive all the love
that is waiting inside the one for me?

reservation for one

I'm tired of being the girl before the wife.

I'm tired of putting in effort
to better the man,
build him up,
hear his story,
write the next chapter for him.

I'm tired of being the girl before the wife.

the one who invests years,
and love,
and tears,
the one who invests with no return.

I'm tired of being the girl before the wife.

only to watch them turn around,
time and time again,
and choose the next girl.

reservation for one

the hardest part about looking for love
and never finding it,
is having to accept that it's not that you
can't find what you're looking for –
it's the fact that what you're looking for
might not exist.

the kindness you yearn for,
the gentle partnership,
the loyalty,
the person who also wants forever –
it could all be a fantasy.

a dream sold to us by movies
and romance novels,
and not something that is real
or attainable.

sure, maybe some people find it
but how many?
certainly not the majority.

and certainly not me.

reservation for one

when you're searching for your soulmate,
your life feels like a waiting room.

everyone's name gets called before you –
the room empties,
one by one,
while you sit there –
still waiting.

every time someone gets their turn,
you grow hopeful
only to feel utter disappointment again.

what started out as a room
full of understanding and empathy
turns into a room full of empty chairs,
a ticking clock,
and you.

reservation for one

you call it *cuffing season*
I call it *single season.*

you're at the pumpkin patch
with your one and only,
I'm at the pumpkin patch
reminded that I'm lonely.

you're burrowed together on the couch
cozy blanket, sipping wine.
I'm swiping left on dating apps,
wondering if that will ever be mine.

you're taking walks in the snow
planning a future that includes a ring,
I'm shoveling my walk myself
feeling the weight of all that's missing.

you have what I want
and am scared I'll never get,
I'm longing for someone
that I haven't even met.

reservation for one

to wish to be desired –
my, how this stings.

to hope that someone will look *at* you
and see you
rather than looking right *through* you.

reservation for one

it feels like love is reserved for other people.

other people get the love story,
the best friend,
the happy ending.

other people don't have to struggle
and beg
and plead
for what feels like a rite of passage for all.

other people look at me like I am peculiar
because I haven't received
everything that they have.

other people have love
fall into their lap
while I search the ends of the earth for it.

it feels like love is for everyone else
and will never be for me.

reservation for one

it's not just being single that's hard.

it's feeling left out of your friend group
when you're the last single friend.

it's attending every bridal lunch,
bachelorette party, and baby shower, and
having nobody show up to cut cake for your
birthday or cheer for your accomplishments.

it's the isolation of your friends planning
weddings together and then gathering up
their babies for play dates, and telling you
we guess you can come, if you want.

it's the annoyance of having to repeatedly
answer *no* when people relentlessly ask if
you've found someone yet, and then the pain
of silence when you notice they stop asking
because they realize your answer will never
be *yes*.

it's being on the fringes. like you're an
outsider to the lives of the ones you thought
you'd walk this journey with.

it's not just being single that's hard.

it's all hard.

reservation for one

when you are single and hoping for love,
triggers are everywhere.

at the mall
couples walk in twos,
holding hands,
making it hard for you to get around them,
and making it hard to forget how cold
your own hand is.

when you are single and hoping for love,
you can step on a landmine at any time.

when you see a couple at the movies,
nestled and laughing together,
sharing popcorn –
sharing a life.

when you are single and hoping for love,
there seems to be nowhere you can turn
that does not remind you
that you are single and hoping for love

reservation for one

I'm worried for the grief
I'll have to face alone.

the eventuality of saying goodbye
to my parents one day,
and not having anyone
to hold my hand through it.

facing my own aging –
my wilting health
and aching body,
and doing it all by myself.

walking towards the end of life
on a path that was always unaccompanied.

I'm worried that as lonely as life has felt,
death will feel even lonelier.

reservation for one

my father tells me
he put aside money for my wedding.

my mother asks me
when I'll give her grandchildren.

they are waiting for me to find love,
just like I am waiting for me to find love.

as disappointed as I feel
to have not found *the one*,
disappointing them feels heavier.

reservation for one

it is a heartbreaking realization
that the love stories you looked up to
and looked forward to –
the fairy tales,
and books,
and movies,
were that and nothing more –
just stories.

destined to live only in pages
and on screens,
and never to be a reality for you.

reservation for one

my heart wanted to believe
that love was coming for me.

so I waited patiently
like a kid waiting to open presents
on christmas eve –
they've never seen santa
but still believe he exists.

there is proof of love everywhere –
people in every corner of the earth
who have found it and stay in it,
so I thought
why not me?

but time passed,
and passed,
and passed,
and it never came for me.

kids grow up and stop believing in santa.

I grew up and stopped believing in love.

reservation for one

I worry that because I want love so badly,
I won't choose well.

that because my heart is so lonely,
I will latch on to the first one
who shows me a sliver of affection.

I worry that the years of solitude
and disappointment
and self-doubt
will damper my discernment.

I worry that I'll forget all that I deserve.

reservation for one

so much of being single
is grief.

grieving the person
you feel like you've lost
though you haven't even met them yet.

grieving the picture of your life
you imagined all these years
which has not come to fruition.

grieving the children you were sure
you would be a mother to by now
and who you are now unsure
will ever be born.

grieving the thought
that the answer might not be *not yet*
but rather,
will be *never*.

reservation for one

have you tried dating apps? / they worked for my friend / you just have to put yourself out there / have you tried smiling more? / I know someone - let me set you up / put on a little bit of makeup to show you care / wipe off some of that makeup – it's too much / it'll happen when you least expect it / you just need to love yourself first / you love yourself too much / you're too independent / men like when you… / men don't like when you… / maybe you're too picky / maybe you expect too much

single women have heard it all

reservation for one

I always thought the pain
would be for something –
that it would render some type of reward.

that the endless swiping
and the blind dates
and the setups I didn't want to say yes to
would lead me somewhere.

but they haven't.

I'm still just as single,
and I'm twice as frustrated.

*is finding love
really supposed to be this hard?*

reservation for one

reminders of my loneliness are everywhere.

reminders are at the grocery store
when I see the couple together,
lovingly squeezing avocados,
choosing the best one –
choosing the best for one another.

planning their dinner
as though it were the most mundane
and regular thing,
when really, it is an enviable display of love.

they are tender with one another
in a way I can only dream of receiving.

reminders are present
when I look out my window
and see the old couple
cautiously helping each other
down the sidewalk.
the years have passed them by
and left them with a lifetime of memories.

reminders of my loneliness are everywhere,
but so are glimmers
of what could be waiting in my future.

maybe one day, that will be me.

reservation for one

I hope that in another life,
I have found love.

I hope that in another life,
I have stumbled upon
the person I am supposed to be with.

we'll have a calm and gentle life,
and a calm and gentle love.

we will be kind to one another –
we will remember each other's coffee orders
and remember each other's triggers.

we will garden in the yard together,
make each other hot cups of tea,
and kiss the tops of one another's heads.

he will check the oil in my car
and I will bake muffins for his work potluck.

it's all so simple –
it's nothing grand, really.
but it's all I ever wanted.

so I'll wait patiently for the next life,
if I have to.

reservation for one

loving yourself enough
won't guarantee that you'll receive the love
of another.

this is a lie propagated
to put the blame back on us
when the blame belongs on the shoulders
of a culture that rewards
shallow relationships.

telling single women that healing
will attract their partner to them
while unhealed people find love every day
is damaging.

it's not your fault.
you do love yourself enough.
and even if you didn't,
you'd still deserve love.

sure, I can buy myself flowers. I can write myself love notes and take myself out on fancy dates – put on that cute dress I've been saving for a special occasion.

I can love myself with an intensity so fierce that I *almost* don't need anyone else to love me. but it would only ever be *almost*.

I still hope for love. for fingers intertwined and good morning texts and *do we need milk? I'm stopping by the store.*

I can love myself and still hope for someone to run my plans by, just in case we already have some of our own.

I can love myself and still wish for the words *we* and *us* to one day be a part of my vocabulary.

I don't need to choose between self-love, and love.

reservation for one

I'm growing tired of berating myself
for not having found love yet.

how can I expect others to be kind to me
when I am so unkind to myself?

I'm growing tired of ignoring
all the blessings around me
simply because I don't have someone
to share them with.

how can the universe love me
when I am overlooking all it has to offer?

2. love in the wrong generation

damn, this loneliness can run so deep.

it feels like you
have missed the boat on love –
like it has sailed away
and is never coming back.

damn, this life can be so hard.

when everyone around you
has someone to walk through it with,
and you are dragging yourself
up the trail alone.

damn, you're stronger than you even know.

you wake up every day
and face the silence head on.

you hold your own hand
and you keep yourself going.

reservation for one

there are days I am strong alone,
and there are days that I am not.

it would be nice to have someone
bring me chicken soup when I'm sick.

it would be nice to have someone
help me build the ikea furniture
that is supposed to be simple,
but never is.

it would be nice to have someone
to kill that spider
(or rather, take it outside)

it would be nice to have someone
who can reach the nutmeg
on the top shelf for me.

it would just be nice to have someone.

reservation for one

you're going to have to sit with yourself.

you're going to have to sit with yourself
and feel every single feeling deeply –
the loneliness,
the grief,
the anger,
the shame.

you're going to have to look those feelings
dead in the eye,
steady your gaze, and say
I'm not scared of you.

reservation for one

I don't want to hear any more advice.

on how to meet my person,
where he might be waiting,
and what I'm doing wrong.

it's exhausting to hear from people
who have already found their forever,
without having to struggle for it.

it's exhausting to hear
all the things they think you're doing wrong
in a challenge they've never had to face.

I don't want to be told I'm too picky,
that I'm making it too complicated,
that I just need to do *this* or *that*.

how would they know?

they've never been in my shoes.

reservation for one

I'm single,
but at least I'm not wondering
where he is at 2 am.

I'm single,
but at least I'm not begging
a grown man to treat me with respect.

I'm single,
but at least I'm not lying to myself
about whose lipstick I found in his car.

I'm single,
but at least I'm not googling his behaviour
and gaslighting myself into accepting it.

I'm single,
but at least I'm not hearing
I don't know what you want me to say
after spilling the contents of my soul to him.

I'm single,
but at least I'm not waiting years for a man
who is still figuring out what he wants.

I'm single,
and it's not the worst thing I could be.

reservation for one

I'm so tired
of showing up to girls dinners
to regale my married friends
with tales of the hellscape that is dating.

I'm so exhausted
from *swiping, swiping, swiping*
and feeling it tear apart my insides,
but having it be fuel
for everyone else's amusement.

I'm so over
yet another crappy first date
that I recap to my best friend on the phone
while she curls up next to her *person* –
the one she didn't have to go through
any of this to find.

I no longer want to smile
and laugh
and make jokes
just to hide the fact that this really hurts.

reservation for one

single cat lady is not an insult.

I should be so lucky.

to have the companionship of myself
and the companionship of a loving creature
after trying in vain to find someone
with a heart as caring as mine.

I should be so lucky.

to have such peace in my life
after hoping for my effort to be matched,
my care to be reciprocated,
and my heart to be handled gently,
only to find that this treatment is rare.

single cat lady is not an insult.

it says more about them
than it does about me
that I'd choose the cat over them
any day.

reservation for one

talking stage.
ghosting.
breadcrumbing.
lovebombing.

these are just words –
terminology to soften the blow.

we have found a lot of indirect ways
to simply say this –
finding love is exhausting.

reservation for one

the next time someone
gives you dating advice
or belittles you for being single,
remind yourself
you don't need to take advice
from anyone who doesn't have
what you want.

just because they're in a relationship
doesn't mean they're in a good relationship.

reservation for one

people ask me all the time
why I am still single.

there's a thousand things I could say.

I don't wish to be half loved.

*I'm always there when I need me,
and I expect the same from others.*

It's hard to find real love in a fake world.

people ask me all the time
why am I still single.

but it's hard to explain
to those who accept crumbs
why I'm waiting for the whole loaf.

when I was a little girl, my friends and I
would tear up old white bedsheets, wrap
them around ourselves, and play *wedding.*

we'd take turns being the bride and walking
down the aisle holding flowers, pretending
to cry happy tears, and saying it was *the best
day of our lives.*

and I truly thought it would be. I thought it
would be my greatest achievement and that
my wedding day would feel like winning the
lottery.

but I didn't realize that in order to win the
lottery, you have to buy a ticket. and that
finding the right person – finding your
soulmate – is about as hard as landing that
winning ticket.

so as I navigate a sea of *I'm not looking for
anything serious* and *let's just be friends
with benefits* I think back to little me and
wonder if that was the only wedding I'll
have in this lifetime.

I'm disappointed for her, but I absolutely
refuse to settle.

reservation for one

just because I haven't found someone
who meets my standards
doesn't mean my standards are too high.

after all,
I meet my standards.

just because you can't,
doesn't mean I should lower them.

reservation for one

they tell me that I am asking for too much
and I cannot help but wonder –

but did you ask for enough?

they tell me
*you just have to pick someone –
anyone at all.*

to the ones who say
it doesn't matter
because they're all the same,
and that it's better to be with someone
than no one,

I want to know -
did they ask for enough?

reservation for one

God's plan for me does not include
waiting all day long for a text back.

God's plan for me does not include
crying into my pillow every night
over being mistreated,
just so I can say I have someone by my side.

God's plan for me does not include
me accepting the bare minimum
while I give everything inside of me.

God's plan for me does not include
having to swallow my pain
when he likes another girl's pictures
and tries to convince me I am wrong
for feeling hurt.

God's plan for me does not include
me having to teach a man what empathy is.

God's plan for me does not include
sacrificing what I know I deserve
simply so I can have a ring on my finger.

reservation for one

I see you, single women.

I see you when you go on group trips and are given the couch to sleep on, while the couples get the comfortable beds in the spacious rooms.

I see you when you show up for your friends bridal showers and weddings with gifts in hand and a smile on your face, but celebrate your own birthdays and career milestones alone.

I see you when you are told *you just need to love yourself* and *it'll happen when you least expect it* while knowing this is trite advice given by those who don't know what else to say.

I see you when your demoralizing dating experiences are turned into "funny" stories on girls nights out, while you pretend to laugh so you don't cry.

I see you, single women.

and I see that you deserve better.

reservation for one

stop waiting for a partner.

buy the house.
go on that trip.
take yourself out to the fancy restaurant –
get the lobster bisque,
get the steak and wine too –
revel in it.

buy tickets to that concert.
dance with your girlfriends.
dance with a stranger.
dance with yourself.

throw dinner parties.
invite your best friends,
take out the good china –
stop saving it for a special occasion.

live.

whether you have someone or not.

you deserve to.

reservation for one

love has changed.

it used to be something respected,
revered,
appreciated.

now it is swiping and hookups,
notches on a belt.

it has become a relic of the past –
like a hundred-year-old painting
that we admire in a museum
while we jump from person to person.

no one is ever good enough –
the search never ends.

we are somehow too picky,
yet unable to pick the right person.

love has changed.

I think I was born in the wrong generation.

reservation for one

alone does not need to mean lonely.

if you know yourself,
see yourself,
honor yourself,

alone will never mean lonely.

reservation for one

here is an ode to the women.

to the women who showed up for me
when I didn't have the strength
to show up for myself.

to the women who remember my birthday,
remember to call me,
remember *me*.

to the women who bring bottles of wine –
laugh with me,
sit with me,
remind me of what kinship is.

to the women who were
there at the beginning,
stayed for the middle,
and will be here still, in the end.

to the women who remind me
that love is found in all forms,
all spaces,
all friendships.

to the amazing women
who help me remember the amazing woman
that I am too.

reservation for one

you tell me to settle down
but somehow,
it feels like you're telling me –
just settle.

reservation for one

it's not enough
to find someone to share your bed with.

and it's not enough
to find someone to share your body with.

it's about finding someone
you can share your soul with.

someone who sees you,
all of you,
and still wants to stay.

reservation for one

when I was 5,
I watched disney movies
and looked forward to finding the prince
to my princess.

when I was 12,
I realized I wanted what my parents had –
someone to wash the dishes with each night
and someone to remember that
I don't like pickles on my burgers.

when I was 16,
I received my first broken heart –
the boy from fifth period history class,
and I realized that sometimes love
leaves us feeling a little emptier.

when I was 25,
I moved my things out of an apartment
I shared with the person
who I thought was the love of my life,
and I realized love isn't always linear.

I have never stopped learning
what love is
and what love isn't.

and I don't think this lesson
will ever be complete.

reservation for one

beautiful things in this life
are still beautiful
without someone by your side.

beautiful things in this life
are still beautiful
with only you as their witness.

reservation for one

dear friend,

I know your priorities have changed.

I know you are a wife and mother now,
and I know you are a wife and mother first.

but I still care for you,
and I still love you.

and the truth is,
I miss you.

I miss conquering the world together,
and I miss looking to the future together.

I miss your phone calls,
movie nights,
the laughter,
our adventures.

I am so happy for you.

but I can be happy for you
while feeling your absence deeply,
and grieving that you have moved on
without me.

reservation for one

maybe the problem is not with me
for being single,

but with society
for making single women
feel like they're the problem.

reservation for one

you can be everything.

you can be a good cook,
smart,
ambitious,
have the corner office with the window,
be soft when needed,
and still not be *chosen*.

so some days,
you're going to have to make
a conscious effort to choose yourself.

some days,
you're going to have to act
like your own partner –
buy yourself your favorite takeout dinner
for no reason at all.

set flowers on the table
so that dinner feels extra special.

give yourself words of affirmation,
and keep choosing yourself
regardless of who does or does not
choose you.

reservation for one

I am not looking for someone
to complete me –
I don't feel incomplete.

I'm looking for someone
who reminds me daily
of just how complete I already am.

reservation for one

I'm always there when I need me
and I can't say the same for others.

so the next time you want to ask
why I am single,
please pause.

instead,
ask yourself –
wouldn't you choose the same?

reservation for one

I am so glad I didn't marry
anyone I've loved in the past.

I am so glad it didn't work out
with anyone whose love
did not feel big enough,
warm enough,
or strong enough
for me.

I am so thankful that I refused to settle.

I am so thankful that I ignored
the snide comments,
the rude questions,
the endless *you're still single?*
at every thanksgiving dinner.

I am so thankful I know what I want.

because this means I'll know it
when I see it,
and it will all have been worth it.

this means that when it comes,
I'll grab it with both hands
and never let it go.

reservation for one

before you choose someone
just for the sake
of having a person by your side,
ask yourself,

can you picture him holding you
while you grieve the certain heartaches
that life hands out –
friends moving away,
the loss of your parents,
aging,
illness.

can you picture him
doing your future daughter's hair –
tenderly combing out the tangles,
tenderly protecting your family.

can you picture him caring for you
when you're sick,
lovingly bringing you bottles of pills,
counting them out,
ensuring you take just the right ones.

before you choose someone
just for the sake
of having a person by your side,
ask yourself,
*what type of person would you like
by your side?*

reservation for one

I spent too long changing myself
in hopes of receiving love.

from now on I'm only loving
the one who loves me
with my glasses on,
my freckles uncovered,
my frazzled state of my mind
when I can't find my car keys.

from now on I'm only loving
the one who holds me
when I can barely hold myself up.

from now on I'm only loving
the one who is committed
to truly seeing me.

from now on I'm only loving
the one who loves me
the same way I love them.

reservation for one

everyone keeps telling me to love myself,
and that this is how I will find my person.

but time has shown me
that I want to love myself for me –
not for anyone else.

not to bring a man into my life.
not to convince society I deserve love.
not to attract anyone else towards me.

I want to love myself
because the greatest act of self-love
is to simply go ahead and do it.

the greatest act of self-love
is to live a life that feels rich and whole
and full of all the things
that fill my cup.

reservation for one

I'm not sure if I want marriage and kids
because it's what I truly want,
or if it's because it's what I'm told
I *should* want.

my sister comes home from work
to cook and clean,
while her husband comes home from work
to watch tv.

my friends chase after their children,
while their husbands stare at their phones.

I'm not sure if I want marriage and kids
like the people around me
have marriage and kids.

I want a different version.

a version that keeps me safe.
a version where I can be happy too.
a version where everyone wins.

and it is crushing to realize
this version may not exist.

reservation for one

I would rather live a life alone,
than regret choosing the wrong person
to give my heart to.

being single is not the scariest thing.

reservation for one

I'm hard to impress.

because for years now,
I've been impressing myself.

I'm hard to impress
because I show up for myself,
on good days and bad,
and I won't accept anything less
from anyone else.

I'm hard to impress
because I see my own beauty
and cannot relate
to those who don't.

I'm hard to impress
because I know how wonderful
my own company is
and I know how lucky anyone would be
to bask in it.

I'm hard to impress
because whoever I choose
to spend time with
is competing with nobody else
but me.

3. I´ll be okay

reservation for one

I've prayed to God
a thousand times
to help me find my person –
to not let this life pass me by
without experiencing love.

I started to question if God
could hear me,
or if perhaps I was praying wrong.
because I'm still praying.
and love still hasn't arrived.

but I'm choosing to keep the faith.

reservation for one

there is no shame in wanting a relationship.
there is no shame in hoping to find
someone to love,
who you can love life with together.

but please,
center yourself while you search.

don't lose yourself in the chase.

reservation for one

maybe there is more to life
than being in a relationship.

maybe there are pictures to paint
and books to write.

flowers to buy yourself
and peace in a quiet moment
with your favorite tv show
and a bowl of pasta.

maybe there are nights
where you take an everything shower,
put on your softest pajamas,
dance around to your favorite songs,
and fall asleep
truly content.

reservation for one

I am not less than
the married women,
the coupled women,
the ones twirling
in beautiful white dresses
with bouquets in hand.

I am not less than
the ones in the park,
toting kids and toys –
a baby on the hip
and a stroller in their path.

I am not less than them.

my life looks different,
but it still holds so much value.

reservation for one

I'm sick of being sad –
In fact I think I'm done.

I'm sick off feeling the pressure
of trying to find *the one.*

because the truth of the matter
is that there's not just one,
there's a million things in this life
and I'm nowhere close to done.

there's thailand and spain,
I could hop on a flight today,
there's friends to make and laughs to share,
there's too much I won't let slip away.

there are books to read,
pages to turn,
there's more to life
than an endless yearn.

so I'm done with being sad
and focusing on the lack,
I'm ready to center myself
and take my own life back.

reservation for one

I don't want just any love –
I want a life changing love.

I want a love that thinks of me first thing in the morning.

I want a love that remembers the stories I've shared about my childhood.

I want a love that holds me up when I'm falling.

I want a love that does the laundry with me without me asking.

I want *I can't wait to see you*'s, and *let me get you seconds – you look hungry.*

because to be loved is to be seen.
and I know I deserve to be seen.

reservation for one

I wasted my youth
wanting someone else
when I could have spent my youth
wanting myself.

I was gorgeous and kind,
funny and smart,
and yet I chased men
like they were the prize.

they weren't the prize – I was.
in fact,
I still am.

I'm still gorgeous and kind,
and I'm still funny and smart.

I refuse to waste even one more day.

reservation for one

I thought I was lonely because I was single.

It turns out this isn't true.

I was lonely because I kept rejecting myself
in pursuit of someone else.

I was lonely because I propped others
up on a pedestal
and lowered myself
as though I were nothing.

I was lonely because I listened to a world
that told me I needed to find someone
and let me forget
that I *am* someone.

reservation for one

maybe love is more than a man.

love can be shoveling your elderly neighbors sidewalk on a snowy day.

love can be calling your parents on a random tuesday afternoon, just to ask them how they're doing.

love can be walking your dog and letting them stop to sniff every flower.

love can be dropping off food on the porch of your best friend who just had a baby.

love can be when you take yourself outside to sit in the sun.

love can be when you find an old birthday card from your grandparents and it feels like they're still right here beside you.

love can be when your friend stops by with homemade cupcakes.

love can be making yourself a cup of warm tea after a long day.

love can be you.

reservation for one

even if I find my soul mate,

he will not be the one
who has been with me from day one,
all the way until my last breath.

that is me.

even if I find my soul mate,
he will not be inside my head,
even if he is inside my heart.

that is me.

even if I find my soul mate,
he won't replace the love
I need to provide for myself.

that will always be my job.

even if I find my soul mate,
I still need to show up for myself.

reservation for one

I am holding on to hope
that he is still coming.

I am holding on to hope
that somewhere out there
is someone who was created
so perfectly for me,
as I was created
so perfectly for him.

this does not mean
either of us are perfect –
for there are no perfect beings.

we are both flawed apart,
and we will both be flawed together.

but our flaws will align,
and we will forgive.

our flaws will complement,
and we will do the work.

because there is no such thing as perfect
but there is such a thing as hope.

reservation for one

maybe we need to stop telling little girls
that marriage is the ultimate goal.

maybe we need to stop telling them
the white dress
or the picket fence
is the best they'll ever do,
and the most important thing to aspire to.

maybe we need to start teaching them
that life has a lot to offer,
and that while the love of another might be
one of those things,
it is not everything.

reservation for one

I was 8 years old
when I watched my parents
slow dance in the kitchen,

my father's hand
on the small of my mother's back.

my mother's eyes
lost in his gaze.

I thought to myself –
I can't wait for that to be me.

they are still dancing.
and I am still waiting.

because of them,
I believe in endless possibilities.

reservation for one

life doesn't end at 30.
and it doesn't end at 38 or 42 either.

you don't need to take part
in this toxic race
that tells us we only have so long
to achieve our dreams.

you don't need to compare yourself
to anybody else,
and you need not compare what you have
to what they have
in order to be happy.

the best is yet to come.

reservation for one

it turns out ending up single
is not my biggest fear.

my biggest fear
is ending up with someone
I settled for.

my biggest fear
is losing myself in a small love
when I always desired a big love.

my biggest fear
is knowing I deserve more
but accepting less.

my biggest fear
is spending my time pursuing someone else
and overlooking myself.

my biggest fear
is missing my own life
and letting it pass me by
because I didn't realize
I've always been the best part of it.

reservation for one

I put too much on romantic relationships.

I forgot that love
is not something I need to seek
or something that someone else
needs to give to me.

I forgot that life is love.

I forgot that I can find love
in a little café,
writing in my journal while drinking a latte,
and drinking in my own company.

I forgot that I can find love
while I sit on a plane
flying towards a foreign country
where I know I'll see sights
I thought I'd only ever see in my dreams.

I forgot that I have love
in my family,
my friends,
the people who show up
with cookies during the holidays,
and the people who call me
just to ask how I am.

love is absolutely everywhere.

reservation for one

being single
does not equal *dying alone.*

water your friendships
and watch a beautiful garden flourish.

nourish your family
and feel the abundance multiply.

pour into yourself
and let your cup overflow.

reservation for one

I owe myself an apology
for forgetting that I am
an extraordinary person
to spend this life with.

I owe myself an apology
for getting lost
in the pursuit of a soul mate
and neglecting the fact
that love lives inside my soul,
and always will.

I owe myself an apology
for seeking a hand to hold
all the while my own two hands
have been building a beautiful life for me.

I owe myself an apology
for forgetting that everything I'm seeking
out there
also lives
in here.

reservation for one

this world hates to see
a happy single woman coming.

she challenges the status quo
and disrupts the very system
they expect her to uphold.

she is not miserable without a man,
and her lack of misery
makes too many others miserable.

this world hates to see
a happy single woman coming.

so be careful –
they're going to try to tear you down.

reservation for one

I'm ready to celebrate more
than the weddings
and more than the babies.

don't get me wrong –
these milestones deserve celebration.

but don't other life events
deserve celebration too?

what about the promotions?
the graduations
where we proudly walk the stage?

what about the divorces –
the *I finally left him - good riddance!*

what about the writing of the books?
and the buying of the houses?
and the
*oh my gosh – did you realize
we've been friends for 10 years now?*

what about *you*?

reservation for one

I fell in love
with the world around me,

and finally stopped agonizing over
falling in love with a man.

reservation for one

when each long day ends,
I have somewhere to rest my head.

I have peace and quiet –
a cozy space to call my own,
delicious food,
freedom to unwind.

I have all the girly things –
a glass of wine,
the shows I like,
crafts and poetry and a comfortable bed.

I can put my feet up –
nobody expects me to pamper them,
when I need so much pampering myself.

it is not all bad.

actually – it's really, really good.

there is so much bliss in my own presence.

reservation for one

some days,
I am *independent woman*
boss babe
needs nobody.

other days,
I think about what life would be like
If I had someone by my side
to share the struggles with.

on all of these days,
I am whole.

and on all of these days
I deserve love.

reservation for one

here's the thing –
I still hope to find love.

loving myself single
does not mean I've abandoned the desire
for tender touches across my cheek
and someone to ride bikes with in the park.

but I've abandoned the notion
that without it, I'm incomplete.

I've abandoned the self-pity
and the expectations.

I've abandoned the attachment
to any particular outcome.

maybe it will happen,
and maybe it won't.

I'll be okay either way.

reservation for one

it's not the worst thing —
to make a reservation for one
and be seated in your own company.

look at the way you can spread out,
take up all the space,
expand,
be you.

you can order what you want,
savor it at your own pace,
watch the people go by,
watch yourself bloom.

it's entirely up to you
whether you invite someone to join you
or not.

but if you do,
promise me only this —
that they will be someone
who will sit down gently,
respect your space,
and respect you.

when they come,
(and even if they don't)
hold on to the joy of sitting with yourself.

Contact:

You can connect with Alia at @aliasummerswrites across all social media platforms, and at aliasummerswrites@gmail.com

Printed in Great Britain
by Amazon